THE GALLERY OF LIGHT

BILLY LAMONT

National Post Modern Publishing
New York

THERE'S NO TRUTH LIKE THE TRUTH
YOU DARE TO LET YOURSELF SEE
BILLYS POETRY LETS YOU SEE
THE TRUTH OF HIMSELF AND
THE TRUTH THAT SURROUNDS HIM
WHICH IS ALSO THE TRUTH THAT SURROUNDS YOU
TAKE A LOOK AND YOU WILL FIND
LOVE, HATE, ALL LIFE IN IT.

Mike Peters
Singer for —

- *I.R.S. Recording Artists The Alarm*
- *Mike Peters And The Poets of Justice*

Dear Reader,

The Gallery Of Light is a compilation of three books that appear as three separate chapters. Ideally each chapter should be read in one sitting in a certain setting.

The Gallery Of Light
was written to be read by candle light.

Protest
should be read in a cafe with a hot cup of coffee.

Eulogy: Flowers For The Living
should be read while sitting in a historical graveyard on a lazy afternoon.

I pray my words are a kiss to your spirit!

Love,

Billy Lamont

— Let love shine like sunlight in your soul

Editor– Huckleberry Metropolis

Proofreading– National Post Modern Publishing Staff

Additional Proofreading– Janine Krziwda, Lew Yedwab

Thank you for your encouragement and support:

Dawn "Butterfly" Bartels, Mom & Dad, Bobby Lamont, John and Anna Bembenek, Billy Poulos, Mike & Barbara Cruz, George Baschuk, Steve Wolf, Gary Comodo, Janine Krziwda, Phil Accardi, Huckleberry Metropolis, Scott Albert, Bob Buchmann, Joe Franklin, Malibu Sue, Dave Kendall, Dave Sharp, Richard and Eileen Bartels, Jerry Rooney, Jeff and Anna Kozyra, Roseanne Bowar, Pastor Robert C. Forseth, Pastor Tom Victor, Pastor Gary Zarlengo, and all at National Post Modern Publishing.

Special Thanks to:
Mike and Julie Peters, and Professor William J. Steedle.

Does anyone care ???
You can write to Billy Lamont–

c/o The Other Perspective Management
P.O. Box 284
Northport, NY 11768

National Post Modern Publishing
JAF Box 7035
New York, N.Y. 10116-7035

Library of Congress Catalog Card Number: 92-61777
ISBN: 0-9632881-0-5

CONTENTS

Photographs

Please support the following organizations:

Amnesty International —

Mission: to abolish torture and to secure the freedom of victims of human rights violations.

In USA:

P.O. Box 37137
Washington D.C. 20013

Greenpeace —

An international organization dedicated to preserving the earth and all the life it supports.

In USA:

1436 U Street, NW
Washington D.C. 20009

Long Island Cares —

Provides emergency food assistance on Long Island and sponsors programs that help families achieve self-sufficiency. This organization was founded by the late folk singer Harry Chapin.

P.O. Box 1073
Brentwood, N.Y. 11717

World Wildlife Fund —

Reaches across continents to threatened lands and endangered animals providing emergency assistance, technical training and strategic leadership.

In USA:

1250 Twenty-fourth Street, N.W.
Washington D.C. 20037

This book is dedicated to Jesus Christ
with deepest gratitude and love.

The Gallery of Light

STROBE LIGHT

an adult lies in the fetal position
in a strobe light generation

addicted to dreams of –
    midnight impulses
    & sugar passions

screaming,
    "my bedroom/a jail cell
    my bedroom/a jail cell"

a baby left in city traffic
getting fitted for a mental straight jacket
a sunflower with a snake at its root
a cherry tree that needs to bear fruit
metaphysical visions of a paraplegic soul

WAX MUSEUM

My memories are like mannequins in a wax museum
Standing frozen
Only to become animated
When I wander through the corridors of my mind

THE POET'S EYE

Your lies are like a mist
I can't see through
My tears are a waterfall
In this river of blood
I am transparent
My heart is made of glass
The truth is fireworks
Going off in the sky
And the guiding lighthouse
Is the poet's eye

Welcome to the gallery of light......

I Spotlight

DOCUMENTARY

We see the world through the lens of a camera
Recording our videotape
And editing out the parts we don't like
And the final movie is our life

THE FUN HOUSE

If you pay the price of admission
The fun house is always filled with laughter
If you're the same as everyone else
And your life is free from disaster

THEATER OF ROSES

the spotlight is too bright tonight
people think I'm acting when I'm on stage
but the pain is real!
can the audience hear me?

how come I am so lonely in such a crowded room?
social solitaire in a theater of roses

I must concentrate on my performance
my mind is wandering

> I have to perform
> With everyone's eyes on me
> Need everyone's applause
> To be what I want to be
> Am I confident and secure?
> Or is it just another flaw
> In my personality

someone once told me I was self-centered
I know I am not
I do not have enough self-esteem
maybe I am self-absorbed but not selfish
there is a difference

words can be like switchblades

I was born to create
a creation that creates
– a curse –

THEATER OF ROSES

(continued)

I am better at performing than living life
am I like Charles Baudelaire's albatross?
    "whose giant wings hinder him from walking"
am I too sensitive to live?

when I am confused and vulnerable
I am easy prey
prey/pray   prey/pray
the Apostle Paul said in *The Bible* —
    "cast off the works of darkness and put on the
     armor of light"
can life be spiritual?

as an adult I still play like children do
I make art
my imagination never dies
it just gets stronger and stronger

I was born to create
a creation that creates
    – a gift –

Albert Einstein said –
    "imagination is better than knowledge"
I like that
I have always created a niche for myself to live in
created my own world
sometimes this scares me
I am afraid I will not find my way back into the real
world – maybe that's okay – reality is not always your
friend –

I am like Franz Kafka's hunger artist –
"who fasts because he cannot find
the food he likes"
is that strange?
or am I just living life artistically?

life is spiritual
– balance –
my life was created
I create my life

life is spiritual
but most people are asleep

Plato said in *The Cave* –
"the bewilderment of the eyes are of two kinds
and arise from two causes, either from coming
out of the light or from going into the light"

the audience –
eyes that are black
eyes that are rainbows
eyes that are daggers
eyes that are roses
eyes that are graveyards
eyes that are candles

look into my eyes –
look into my soul

I am an enigma to be gazed upon
analyzed
psychoanalyzed
always to be applauded
but never to be loved

HOUSE OF MIRRORS: A WAY OF LIVING

house of mirrors –

> vanity/vanity/vanity
> my world is a reflection of me

a way of living –

> mask of tragedy/mask of comedy
> blindfolded walkers
> never see light

PERIPHERAL VIEW

We are slaves of passion
Tied to one another by habit

A DREAM OF SOCRATES

The beginning of wisdom
Is realizing how little we know
Then we can push beyond ourselves
And start to grow

MICROWAVE ROMANCE

I love you . . .
from the bottom of my…
current frame of reference

Of course in a few years…
I could have…
a new preference

II Moonlight

i can smile
for family and friends
for a little while

when I'm alone I can't hide the pout
when I'm alone the tears come out

how can I speak when my mind doesn't want
to learn?
how can I walk when I don't know which way
to turn?

STRANDED AT SEA

The waves are pounding my lifeboat
I'm struggling just to stay afloat
My sanity is drifting
As the tide is shifting

I guess I'll always be stranded at sea
Outside of society it gets so lonely . . .
Lonely
It gets so lonely

Darkness surrounds me
The wind howls like a ghost
And ashes on the water
Ashes on the water

Now stranded in a sea so vast
I am an outcast
I am an outcast
I am an outcast!

I guess I'll always be . . .
Stranded at sea

Love is a gas mask in the poison smog

EMOTIONAL VAMPIRES

My words are screaming from my spirit . . .

Emotional vampires
Suck your blood
Drain your soul
Feed off of your desire
All to fill their castle with power
All to build their own private empires
They're emotional vampires

A DAGGER

like a dagger in my heart
buried to the hilt
there's nothing more painful
than guilt

THE DUNGEON OF SIN

Never taking that final step
Spiral staircase made of stone
Gasping for every breath
Air of death in the dark alone

You won't trap me in your
Dungeon
Of sin

Please man put that needle away
I know life is getting rougher
Please man put that gun away
There's always someone t…t…t…tougher

I don't want to teach
I don't want to preach
I just want to reach you

Resuscitation not condemnation!

The streets always stay the same
But you can change.

ADDICTED TO MEDIOCRITY

I am not content to just exist
Will I fly free
Or will the problems persist?
Addicted to mediocrity

Narcissism is a lack of maturity
Emotional infancy
It gives birth to co-dependency
Addicted to mediocrity

Soul censorship will make my history
Human love has its parameters
Spiritual love knows no boundary!
I've been addicted to mediocrity

POLARITY

Material or spiritual?
Temporal or eternal?
Empathy or apathy?
A blessing or a curse?

Fear is faith in reverse!

EVIL

←

→

LIVE

A QUESTION MARK

the video camera spins out of control
the television screen does a vertical roll
the future is a question mark
the future is still a question mark
? ?

television red paint slowly drips down the pale
expressionless mannequin face

* * *

we are all parhelia. bright colored spots of light
on a solar halo

* * *

the scapegoat of your misery is baptized with tears.
salt & light

* * *

sweating blood in the name of love in the endless
black tunnel we call night

III Candle Light

INSECURITY

Is it a visual image?
Or is it a mirage?
You're a master of illusion
Hiding behind your facade

Is it a visual image?
Or is it a mirage?
And can you see beyond
Your little pink corsage

Insecurity!
Your eyes are looking through me
Insecurity!
If you only knew me
Insecurity!
Your eyes are looking through me
Insecurity!
I am a mystery!

My heart is as deep as the deep blue sea
But can you see what's inside of me?

You *lie* here and bask
But I can't love a mask
You hide under covers
I can't do with temporary lovers

INSECURITY
(continued)

Is it a visual image?
Or is it a mirage?
Either way I won't bow down
To your false gods!

Hear the call!
Echoing in this hall
Hear the call!
Echoing in us all

What's inside of me?
What's inside of me?
Insecurity . . . insecurity
Lord . . . deliver me
Lord . . .
Deliver me
I want to reveal
Not conceal
The love that's inside of me

The trumpets are sounding
My heart is pounding
My hands are shaking
Is she faking?
Is she staring?
Am I being overbearing?
Your eyes are looking through me
Insecurity

REALIZATION

the candle of love can burn on into eternity
the flame cannot be extinguished by others
a young lover's eyes turn glassy
realizing…
only by neglect
can the infinite light be dimmed

THE OTHER PERSPECTIVE

I try to be objective
But everything is so subjective
And the choices are too few
And can only be seen from one point of view

In the university of life
I've run out of electives
I'm just living by . . .
The other perspective

Beware of those who watch the parade of souls

with microscope eyes of judgment

PURPLE BRAIN

X-ray mind
Taste my thoughts
And tell me is it the flavor of truth?

A hymn in the wind
Angelic choir
Thoughts meant to inspire
Holy fire

Oh Lord renew my mind
And paint it purple
purple . . .
purple . . .

purple brain

A CROWN OF THORN

Hazy mist on crystal sea
Scarlet sin nailed to a tree
Through your blood we're sanctified
On the altar of souls death crucified

Crown of life, a crown of thorn
Violet spirit newly born
Light shines through shrouded mystery
Risen lamb fulfills ancient prophecy

a spiritual fetus
spins
in a whirlpool of color
a myriad of revelations

open eyes/open eyes/open eyes

a baby's first breath
an old man's death

soul magnet

how can a man be born when he is old?
when he is born of fire
how can a man be born when he is old?
when he is born of water
how can a man be born when he is old?
when he is born of the Spirit

NO VERTIGO

life as an experiment

innocence/experience

do not fear superstitions -
run without inhibitions

walking
barefoot

there are two angels
to every one demon*

standing
naked

free
to
dance

the ravens fly from the tower

light
attracts
light

smile butterfly!

white
rose
on
fire

the pupil of the eye constricts

the
snake
is
dead

NO VERTIGO

*according to *The Bible* one-third
of the angels fell from glory
with Satan and became demons

Our lives are but a fraction of eternity

$$\frac{1}{\infty}$$

A MAZE OF DOORS

There's so much sickness
But only one cure
There's only one way out
In this maze of doors

Faith is a burning candle
In a heart that is pure
And there's only one way out
In this maze of doors

Jesus Christ!

IV Sunlight

MY GOD IS NOT A CONSERVATIVE!

God is different things
To different people:
A light in an alleyway
A cross on a steeple

But my God is not a conservative!
He's an artist!
He painted the sky and rainbows
He sculpted the mountains
He's creative; He created the whole world

My God is not a conservative!
He's an artist!
Better than Michelangelo
Better than Van Gogh
Better than Picasso
Better than Warhol!

THE CULT OF ART

This is the cult of art
In the underground theater

– Friends are people with the same hang-ups
– Children are living their parents' mistakes
– Clubs are malls where people go
  to window-shop for lovers
– 42nd Street is where people rent
  other people's bodies
– Make-up can't make a personality pretty
– Perfume can't make lies smell like the truth
– Sensitivity is intelligence of the soul
– Poetry is therapy!

There are innovators
And there are imitators
Boycott the counterfeit!
Sample the original!

This is the cult of art
In the underground theater

FLOWER FACES

Dance to the rhythm of thought

Color clouds
you were loved before you were born

Flower faces
your soul is one of a kind

Angel kisses
your life is precious

Love bath
learn to love yourself
& then you will be able to love others

See with the eyes of angels!

THE BLUEPRINT OF THE SPIRIT

The passionate
Decode my message:

Patience
Stillness
Balance
Endurance
Laughter
Rest
Meditation

I'm speaking in tongues
A riddle
Decode my message:

A whisper in the Spirit
Is the blueprint of life

SILHOUETTES

When a revelation from the Spirit
Ignites a fire in your heart
Which illuminates a vision
– sheds light on darkness –
Only then gray turns to
Black   and   white
A contrast
So distinct
Silhouettes appear

soul metamorphosis
crucifixion
& resurrection
a poet that is a poem
the subconscious
sunlight
love conquers hate

THE ART OF LOVE

Mirror eyes
You radiate
Watercolors
The softness of your gaze
The art of love
I'm a pioneer in the frontier of your mind
I'm an astronaut floating in your space
I'm a scuba diver exploring your secrets
Mirror eyes
You're my soul mate

CIRCLE

Love is a circle
A bond that cannot be broken
Trust is a feeling
A vow left unspoken

THE GALLERY OF LIGHT

I paint your portrait in my mind
And hang it in the gallery of light
Ultraviolet light
Neon light
Candle light
Like a moth I'm attracted to the light
Our abstract emotions
This surrealistic love
I've got a library of disappointments
But I've got a mansion filled with dreams

Protest

PROTEST

This is my philosophy:
True heroes are not celebrities
True heroes are not socialites in chic bars
True heroes are not yuppies in fancy cars
True heroes are clothed in humility
True heroes are workers for charities

Listen to this prophecy
I am going to war on poverty!
It's time for a revolution!

I am an activist
And in my heart I wave a protest sign
That reads, "To be a leader
Is to be a servant of mankind"

ENVIRONMENTAL TERRORISM

toxic waste
acid rain
big business greed and neglect
the greenhouse effect

tropical rain forests bulldozed
no conservation
animals murdered by poacher's bullets
wildlife extinction

raping the sky
and waging war on creation
is a sick science fiction movie evolution
you ask me to drink from your fountain of wisdom
and it's water pollution
environmental terrorism

I pray for a revolution of love
I pray for a revolution of hope
militant pacifism

all creation will be one –
when the land of my father
is the land for my son

love the sky
make peace with the earth!

HYPNOTIZED BY TV

Pardon the intrusion
On your seclusion
But you're living . . . living an illusion

You try to hide
Behind TV Guide
But you're empty . . . empty inside

HYPNOTIZED BY TV
You can't even see me!
HYPNOTIZED BY TV
You're neglecting your family!
HYPNOTIZED BY TV
Oh passive society!
HYPNOTIZED BY TV
I want you to look at me
But you're looking like a zombie
zombie . . . Zombie . . . ZOMBIE!

False sense of security
Covering immaturity
You can't even see . . . see reality

You have no control
Your senses are getting dull
Can you get that through your thick skull!

HYPNOTIZED BY TV
You can't even see me!
HYPNOTIZED BY TV
You're neglecting your family!
HYPNOTIZED BY TV
Oh passive society!
HYPNOTIZED BY TV
I want you to look at me
But you're looking like a zombie
zombie . . . Zombie . . . ZOMBIE!
You're Hypnotized By TV

I want to make history
Not watch it on TV!!!

COINS IN A PAPER CUP

A democracy
Is a bureaucracy
When those in authority
Don't represent the majority

The subways stink of piss
And the homeless lie lifeless
Trash can clothes
Grocery cart closet
Alleyway bedroom

A recession
Is a depression
When the workingman with the blue collar
Sweats blood for an extra dollar
And still can't feed and clothe his family
In a hopeless economy

A recession
Is a depression
When trying to get ahead
Is like running in a revolving door
Like someone once said,
"The rich get richer
And the poor get poorer"

Politicians practicing nepotism
As they tell me, "Don't fight the system"
A system where you need money to succeed
A system that promotes corporate greed
A system that overlooks the people who are in need

A democracy
Is a bureaucracy
When those in authority
Don't represent the majority

This is the first poem I ever wrote (14 years old)

Proverbs 31:30
"Charm is deceptive, and beauty is fleeting; but a woman who fears the Lord is to be praised."

– *The Bible* –
New International Version

YOU'RE JUST AS BEAUTIFUL

You're sixteen and sweet
Tossing and turning in your sleep
Knowing in your heart
Beauty is only skin deep

Romance and dreams
But sometimes it seems
Love is for others

They say seeing is believing
But looks are always so deceiving

Just like you can't judge a book by its cover
You have hidden treasure and will discover
You're just as beautiful
And a shy girl will one day be a lover
You're just as beautiful
A personality like yours is rare
And you know baby I'll always care
You're just as beautiful
You're just as beautiful to me

Still innocent and pure
As you've gotten older
Knowing beauty in the Lord's eyes
The Beholder

Styles and trends
And pleasing your friends
Still not the answer

They say seeing is believing
But looks are always so deceiving

Just like you can't judge a book by its cover
You have hidden treasure and will discover
You're just as beautiful
And a shy girl will one day be a lover
You're just as beautiful
A personality like yours is rare
And you know baby I'll always care
You're just as beautiful
You're just as beautiful . . . to me . . .

Every rhyme has its reason
And every flower has its season

SIMPLE THINGS

Life is a series of moments . . .
An intimate dinner by candle light
Watching the stars at night
A fire to warm the winter chill
An ambition to fulfill
A moment to lie still

Nothing like a day without a care
A breath of fresh air
. . . simple things

We take a walk
I flirt, you tease, we talk
Hand in hand in the park
Sitting by the ocean after dark

Careless wandering
Endless pondering
We enjoy the simple things
We enjoy the simple things

Every time life becomes too much for me
And I just can't cope
I see the sunrise
In your eyes
And it gives me new hope

At dawn
A new day is born

Holding your hand
Means a lot to me
Being held gently
Means a lot to me
Being kissed tenderly
Means a lot to me
. . . simple things

Let's run away!
And find our own special place
Where we can play
With sunlight on our face

Sweetheart, you are the inspiration for this poem
Baby, You are my home!

Everything in this world is temporal
but love is eternal!
LOVE IS ETERNAL!
And your love is beautiful to behold
Something for me to cherish as we grow old

Life is a series of moments . . .
Going to church on Sunday
Holding you close as we pray
The creation of a dream
The taste of ice cream
Righting a wrong
Listening to a favorite song
Being with family and friends – TO BELONG –

SIMPLE THINGS
(continued)

The feeling of rain
The healing of pain
Exploring a new path
Taking a warm bath
To laugh

Life is a series of moments . . .
Moments I want to spend with *you*

Careless wandering
Endless pondering
We enjoy the simple things
We enjoy the simple things

You want to know what makes it all worthwhile
The secrets in a child's smile
LIFE ITSELF IS A GIFT!

Pride is negative energy

Dignity
& confidence
is healthy

Be humble and follow your dream
And don't let anyone
ever
steal your self-esteem!

Based on the anonymous story of the same name

FOOTPRINTS IN THE SAND

Suddenly!
My life passed before my eyes
Standing alone on the beach
My heart silently cries

Two sets of footprints
The afterlife and its hidden key
One set for my Lord
And one set just for me

Scenes of my life are like
Footprints in the sand
Worst times of my life, my Lord
One set of footprints in the sand
Why did you desert me?
Why didn't you hold my hand?
Why did you desert me?
Why didn't you place your rock
So I could stand?

You said you would never leave me
Each and every day
You said just believe me
And I'll walk with you all the way

But when I was walking
You were nowhere around
I listened for your voice
And could not hear a sound

Scenes of my life are like
Footprints in the sand
Worst times of my life, my Lord
One set of footprints in the sand
Why did you desert me?
Why didn't you take me by the hand?
Why did you desert me?
Why didn't you place your rock
So I could stand?

"I would never desert you, my dear child
Never leave my sheep on their own
When you saw one set of footprints
And were feeling all alone

My precious, precious child
It was then I carried you
My precious, precious child please understand
It was then I carried you"

FIGHT TO THE DEATH!

Trickery!
Anxiety!
Profanity!
Jealousy!
. . .is killing me!

Lust . . . Lust . . . Lust . . .
Pornography

Greed . . . Greed . . . Greed . . .
Love of money

Pride . . . Pride . . . Pride . . .
Vanity

Sin . . . Sin . . . Sin
Idolatry

I'll fight to the death!
Fight to the death!
I'll resist the force of sin
Until my dying breath
I'll fight!

Steal . . . Steal . . . Steal . . .
Robbery

Lies . . . Lies . . . Lies . . .
Hypocrisy

Hate . . . Hate . . . Hate . . .
Bigotry

Fear/Death . . . Fear/Death
Sorcery

You won't take me down!
You won't take me down!
Sin is death; a prison cell
You won't take me to Hell
I'll fight!

I won't take the mark of the beast
I'll be at the Lamb's wedding feast

You have ears to hear
Now hear it:
You can beat me
You can stone me
You can kill the body
BUT YOU CANNOT KILL THE SPIRIT!

TESTIMONY

I've been a man of many faces
And these eyes have seen many places

But when I became a man
I put away childish things
And I turned around to find
The King of Kings

I'm a man but like a child now I'm free
I love you Lord with all my heart and with sincerity
I'm a man but like a child now I'm free
Don't want to hear no foolish wise man's philosophy
Don't want no poor rich man's treasury
Don't want the place of honor like the Pharisees
I just want to love you Lord with all my heart
and with sincerity...

And I know if I were the only man in the whole world
You would have hung on that bloodstained tree
And I know if I were the only man in the whole world
You would have rose from the dead in victory
And I know if I were the only man in the whole world
You would have done it all for me

I've always tried to say the way I feel
And I've always tried to be a person that is real

Now looking out through your eyes
Loving everyone I see
Hoping you can look deep in my eyes
And see your love in me

I'm a man but like a child now I'm free
I love you Lord with all my heart and with sincerity
I'm a man but like a child now I'm free
Don't want to hear no foolish wise man's philosophy
Don't want no poor rich man's treasury
Don't want the place of honor like dignitaries
I just want to love you Lord with all my heart
and with sincerity...

And I know if I were the only man in the whole world
You would have hung on that bloodstained tree
And I know if I were the only man in the whole world
You would have rose from the dead in victory
And I know if I were the only man in the whole world
You would have done it all for me

I just want to love you Lord with all my heart
and with sincerity . . .
This is my testimony

Eulogy: Flowers
for the Living

THE POLITICS OF BEING ME

Is this ministry of information
Just a relic in my memory?
Or a work of priceless art
On display
In the museum of my heart?
The politics of being me

My message and its reception
Is based upon your experience and perception
Everyone lives within their own reality
Not everyone finds their spirituality
I'm climbing the stairs of loyalty
The politics of being me

IDEALS AND WHAT IS REAL

Searching for the truth
Turning 'round like a wheel
The soul is a spiritual mirror
Deciding what is real

Everyone reaches for their dream
Looking to an ideal
Life is a balance beam
Deciding what is real

Moods and attitudes
Ideals and what is real

WORD SCULPTURE

Having the last laugh
Workers on strike
No jobs
Beauty
Valleys
Trees
Seas
Old age
Sensitive heart
A band of gypsies looking for a home
Covenant
Death and the grave
A cave of darkness
Hell or Paradise?
Tortured youth
James Dean
Graffiti
Leather jackets
Chameleon
Passion
Ulterior motives
Linguistics
Word sculpture
Body language
A puzzle
Narcissistic
Electric reality
The skeletons in my closet
Hallelujah!
Blood on the wall
Irony

Schemes
Extremes
Dreams
A voice in the wilderness
Society needs a scapegoat
My God is not a conservative!
No common sense
Blood on the mercy seat
Foreshadowing
Poetic license
Reflections in the mirror
Shadows on the wall
Intimidate
Manipulate
Theology
Ideology
Criticize
Analyze
Input
Output
Self-image
A question mark
Ideas spark
Stress
Escape
Pushing the wrong buttons
Information overload
The cold war
Pioneers explore
Stream of consciousness
Brainstorming
Peace!

A GAME OF CHESS WITH LOVE

Holding me in check
What are you trying to prove?
No one watching my back
Waiting for your next move

Lovers are your pawns
Jokers are in your hand
Though they smile they don't live
In the trail of blood in the sand

Playing a game of chess with love
The Cupid never wanted to play
Playing a game of chess with love
Merlin sculpts you a face of clay
Playing a game of chess with love
The Reaper will not get his pay!

Standing here in check
What are you trying to prove?
The knight watched your back
Too valiant to make a move

My friends are my army
Minstrels are everywhere
And tell me what you do
Waiting for your next move

Playing a game of chess with love
The Cupid never wanted to play
Playing a game of chess with love
Merlin sculpts you a face of clay
Playing a game of chess with love
The Reaper will not get his pay!

WINTER PEACH

Love makes it safe to give in to desire
But should romance be a guiltless fire?
Burning down my home
While forever was a nontransparent speech
To a heart as unripe as a winter peach

STALEMATE

Rush! Rush!
Answer the phone
Oh no!
No mind of their own
We're suppressed
Oppressed
Depressed
All alone
So I'm rejected
Sorry! Disconnected

A game of chess with love
Stalemate!
Jokes and jokes
Laugh, laugh
We disagree
Debate
Sarcastic or sincere?
A smile or a tear?
Work and work
Frozen state
Turn around
Uh oh! I'm late
For my date
With fate

What did I say?
Too fast
Didn't last
Take 2
Right on cue

Change the slate
New date

Newspapers got a front page story
They've got to act
Public disclosure
Of private facts

You played your cards
You bet
You never won yet
Russian Roulette

I need overtime
I need a dime
I need a rhyme
Pay the bills
Uh oh! No frills

I play my guitar
Not getting far
Uh oh! Have to wait
For my date
With fate

Move your pawns
Checkmate!
Jokes and jokes
Laugh, laugh
You rate
Get a promotion
Go out of state

STALEMATE

(continued)

They smile, smile to your face
They talk, talk behind your back
Don't laugh, laugh with me
They laugh, laugh at me

Slander, libel
Lie, gossip
You little snip
I'll crack the whip

10 degrees longitude
20 degrees latitude
Sometimes the way you move
Depends on your attitude

To climb the ladder of success
I have to do better
Than the rest
I have to do better
Than my best

I need a plaid suit
I need a plastic smile
I need short hair
To go anywhere

I'm very tense
But I'm making a lot of sense
I can't relax
For public disclosure
Of private facts

I'm walking barefoot on pointy tacks
I'm walking around with a knife in my back

I rush to the elevator
I run to the escalator
To tip the waiter
Everyone pays their dues
Sooner or later

Publicity men have their contact books
Schoolgirls have their dirty looks
And every song must have a hook

Your love is counterfeit
You are a hypocrite
A game of chess with love
Stalemate!

Changing times
Still making rhymes
Still playing guitar
Still not getting far

Surprise, surprise
We're civilized
Electric eyes
White lies
Green envy
Green money
Blue skies
Today's hellos
Are tomorrow's good-byes

PREJUDICE: A DISEASE WITH NO VACCINE?

Nigger, Honkey, Spick
Heini, Guinea, Mick
I'm sick and tired of prejudice!

Prejudice! A disease with no vaccine?
Prejudice! The worst plague ever seen!
Prejudice! This world should be quarantined!
Prejudice! A wound we've got to clean!

The future takes us back
To our history
To learn
Lesson one:

We can kill with The Bomb
Or a gun
Or words filled with deadly poison
From our tongue

Degradation
Segregation
It's a lack of education!

Sticks and stones
Will break my bones
But words are deadlier
In the mouths of clones

Commie, Polock, Spook
Red, Chink, Gook
Homo, Queer, Dyke
Wop, Hebe, Kike

Is this what you want me to be?
Or is it hype?
Is it me you hate?
Or your own stereotype?

Prejudice! A disease with no vaccine?
Prejudice! The worst plague ever seen!
Prejudice! This world should be quarantined!
Prejudice! A wound we've got to clean!

Don't know much but one thing I know
A baby crawls before he walks
Don't know much but one thing I know
A wise man thinks before he talks

WONDER

I guess I can never be content
Just as a child is so innocent
With knowledge of this world, purity has left
This is not to reason, this is a theft

Why, when I begin to ask a question
People feel very threatened and begin to lie?
And when they are confronted with the truth
It always hurts and they always cry?
I always wonder why

Why are we not brought up to ask questions?
Why are the wrong people always in elections?
Why does it rain and thunder?
Why does it? I always wonder.

I observe what I've been taught
My teachers are not as righteous as they thought
I can see inside their souls
And ask what has it bought?
I always wonder why

Why are we not brought up to ask questions?
Why are we guided with wrong directions?
Does a wise man never blunder?
Does he? I always wonder

THE WORLD IS COMING TO AN END

No matter how far I walk on the beach
Or how far I may reach
The Beatles are gone
And so is John

I have this dream
That mankind can be a team
And feed the poor
Have peace not war

I long for the day when our ruler won't be the gun
And the only thing that will still shine is the sun
The world is coming to an end
Everyone's knees will bend

When will they learn to separate
Church and state
Ripley's Believe It Or Not
The Pope's been shot

He who lives by the sword
Shall die by the sword
Truth comes like a lion
Jesus is Lord

I long for the day when our ruler won't be the gun
And the only thing that will still shine is the Son
The world is coming to an end
Everyone's knees must bend

A STRING OF PEARLS

Pearls are words
Words are art
Art is imagination
Imagination is creation
Creation is life
Life is experience
Experience is wisdom
Wisdom is love
Love is a string of pearls

RED POOL OF PASSION

A king stands in authority
Eyes filled with undying love
Blazing thorny crown
Aura as gentle as a dove

Looking through the glass veil
Into the Garden of Paradise
The burning fire in my heart
Melts my facade like ice

Red pool of passion
Flooding rain of pain
Infinite eyes of compassion
I'll never be the same

You looked in the window of my soul
Reality sets in with a chill
You unlocked the door to my heart
Awakening love lying still

Jesus is the key
A circle in a square
And faith is the bridge
Between the here and there

Red pool of passion
Flooding rain of pain
Infinite eyes of compassion
I'll never be the same
I'll never be the same!

BLUE IMAGINATION

As dark as the night
Darkness is damnation
As white as light
Light is your salvation

There's pure inspiration
In your red resurrection
There's a new revelation
In my blue imagination

In my heart are the colors of the rainbow:
Red
Blue
Yellow
Orange
Green

There's pure inspiration
In your red resurrection
There's a new revelation
In my blue imagination

SENSITIVITY

Your aura is like the smell of roses

Sensitivity . . .
The fragrance of light
The color of sound
The texture of breath
The flavor of fire
The tonality of love

PUPPETS IN THE PARK

Here I stand
Left of center
With rebels in the underground
Experience is my mentor

Social homicide
Is emotional suicide
Where freedom of choice
Has no voice

I won't sell my mind into slavery
I won't be a prisoner to the masses
My eyes can see
I don't need glasses

There are too many
Puppets in the park
There are too many
Puppets in the park

Tradition versus change
The normal versus the strange

There's a war going on in my mind
But I've signed a treaty
And in my diary
I saw a message through the graffiti

I'm the artist living on extremes
As the poet in me dreams

I don't subscribe to your personal grief
I won't give in to the master thief
I'm a martyr every day
Dying... dying...
Dying for my beliefs

There are too many
Puppets in the park
There are too many
Puppets in the park

EULOGY: FLOWERS FOR THE LIVING

Give me my flowers while I'm living
Not when I'm dead
Because in this world sometimes
My heart bleeds crimson red

I'm no preacher
But my pulpit is my life
Laughing through the good times
And wrestling with my strife

I am not afraid to die
Funerals are for the living
Death...what seems like the end
Is only the beginning

"Everything will be okay"
Relatives you don't know handing you bouquets
"It's better this way"
Mourners handing you clichés

Give me my flowers while I'm living
Not when I'm dead
Because in this world sometimes
My heart bleeds crimson red

I'm no preacher
But my pulpit is my life
Laughing through the good times
And loving my wife

Sometimes in life you need a purpose
Like following the Son
Sometimes in life you need no purpose
Just to have fun

Man is not only a physical entity
But also a spiritual being
Death... what seems like the end
Is only the beginning

At the gate Jesus stands in white
Holding your hand just like in life
Taking you to the other side
Following the Angel of Light

Like jumping into a cool stream
Like waking up from a dream
And finding yourself born into a new world
And wiping the sleep from your eyes:

No more tears
No more lies
No more questions
No more alibis
No more sickness
No more compromise
No more death
No more good-byes

Don't put flowers on my empty grave
Cast your tears into the blue ocean
On the next wave

ABOUT THE AUTHOR

Long Island´ born poet Billy Lamont has performed on national television and national radio including the *Joe Franklin Show* on WOR-TV and the syndicated *Religion And Rock* program recorded at WBAB radio. Lamont has given poetry readings throughout the United States and in Europe. His performances combine his poetry with rock music and performance art. Lamont was singer/lyricist for the rock band Walk On Water before it disbanded in 1990. He wrote and performed in their music video *A Game Of Chess With Love* which aired on a number of cable television networks. Lamont's first book of poetry, a chapbook entitled *Eulogy: Flowers For The Living* was published in 1990 and received underground success in the northeast of the United States.